RENEWING THE LIGHT

RENEWING THE LIGHT

COLIN ARCHER

PETERLOO POETS

First published in 1998
by Peterloo Poets
2 Kelly Gardens, Calstock, Cornwall PL18 9SA, U.K.

© 1998 by Colin Archer

**A catalogue record for this book is available
from the British Library**

ISBN 1-871471-74-5

Printed in Great Britain by
Antony Rowe Ltd, Chippenham, Wilts.

ACKNOWLEDGEMENTS:

'Gibberish' first appeared in *The Indepentent* and in the National Autistic Society anthology *A Squillet of Wise Fool's Gold*.

'Beyond Westminster Bridge', which won the 1994 Rhyme International Competition, first appeared in *Orbis*.

'Night Line' first appeared in the Samaritan anthology *Listening Lines*.

'Grannycraft' in *Writers on the Loose*.

'Pastoral', 'Journeys' and 'The Traveller' have appeared in *Other Poetry*.

'Gloria' and 'House Hoard' in *Iron*.

'Memorabilia' in *Poetry Nottingham*.

Other poems have appeared in various competition anthologies.

For Joan

Contents

Renewing the Light

Precarious on the top rung
I spray the winter-filthy outsides as,
feet-firm on the bedroom carpet,
you spray the insides, pane for pane.

Our soft cloths shadow each other
then criss-cross at will; fingernails
pick at the same mark: my mote, your beam;
my half-scowl returning as your half-smile.

I am instantly double-visioned:
frothy blue sky projected onto the screen
between us and, over your shoulder,
colour-washed in clean light, our duvet.

You step back to inspect results, point to
what? where? I lean backwards; you panic,
but I'm still here, holding tight,
and it's simply a blip under the surface.

So many times without a fall; glass intact;
smears coming to light only briefly
in low late sun, banished soon enough
by duller days, plain time, ordinary grime.

Descent

for Niku

Crawling fast and loose, you nose around
the bottom stair, reach up to fumble the pile,
then flail podgy knees until, by half chance,
you take your triumphant first step up.

My vast hands are cupped an inch behind
your tenderpad bottom as you lift your eyes
to the second stair, attempt an encore,
turn your head — and slither back to the start,

only to resume next day, persevere,
steadily win a few more lucky footholds
and, in no time at all, surprise the landing
and confront all those closed doors.

I am still behind you, thinking now
about your Grand Aunt Kit who could, in the end,
only manage stairs on her knees like you
then kept forgetting what she had gone up for.

Meanwhile, you decide to crawl back down —
head first. I scoop you up and turn you round,
but you twist back and launch yourself again
into the void, into the crook of my arm.

Listen, love, you can't come down the same way
you came up. Don't try to look where you're going.
You must learn somehow to *feel* your way.
I turn you yet again: you still don't understand.

Lingering

Tucked into your first full-size bed,
feet squirm towards a too-far-distant end,
find nothing, squabble, then curl back
into a duck-down womb of your own making —

a new dream-space, open to my stories,
songs, love; but losing *touch*,
baffled by the full-blown duvet
and the slow stretch of your imagination.

Once again I too cling to bed-time, drag it out,
wanting to slip into your sleep,
be near to see you straight,
shoo away your waiting nightmares —

and have you there to shame mine. I am troubled
by half-absences, by the unfilled time
I can't yet quite claim; know I should
slip away, leave you to sleep, grow us up.

Journeys

As my daughter clings to the awkwardness
of the camel, my lens ranges past the zoo
to her earliest remembered journey —
before we straddled her on the mute collie
or steered the pram on her first proud lap,
before we even cradled her home.

Throughout that nine-month Odyssey,
the safest hydro-lastic suspension
cushioned her against all the motion of the world —
the stop-start, pitch-roll, tilts and twists,
as day after day she was heaved and humped
towards the bumpy slide and final ejection.

Travel weary, she slept for months,
laid gently on her side to recover
before she could fumble her limbs back to life —
but now she leaps wildly down to my arms,
wriggles her way out, terrifying us
as she bounces off into her own world.

Child-ery

Child-ery is staying away for a night,
stopping up wickedly late, sharing
a strange bathtub. It is the smell
of another child's bedclothes, a giggle
in a rumpled-together tent, sleeping
with somebody else's teddy, waking
in the dark, not quite sure who you are.

Child-ery in the morning is being handed
the wrong socks, getting away with a lick
and a promise, nibbling at a peculiar
cereal. *Child*-ery is a suspicious cat;
a garden with undiscovered hidey-holes;
great games with the vaguest of rules;
different words for the same things.

In the heat of the day, *child*-ery
is bouncing about on top of fizzy drinks,
telling the lady with the soft-centres
that you love her more than anyone else
in the whole world, gobbling up lots of
second helpings. It is a funny pain inside;
having a lovely time — and wanting home.

Gloria

Still you fascinate me
lying in the graveyard
though you never lived
I would have loved you.

Blonde and lusty
is the image
carved on my mind
weathering years.

Long ago my youngest
showed me your name
and asked how it was
that you could lie

   with so many men
O promiscuous daughter
of the lamented
Mr Deo.

How cautious I am
to love the unattainable
and soiled.

Number 76

Dusty sunshine rises from the privet,
the lawn threadbare, concrete birdbath
empty.

My letterbox-rattle echoes
until I surprise a key in my pocket
and break in.

Stark floorboards complain. My breath
disturbs the embrocation of years
from flock wallpaper.

She is still here, somehow left behind
in the kitchen, beside the Aga,
hovering

   in her flowered pinny. Her words
forgive, her ash-serious face
accuses,

my mouth suddenly acid-yellow.

Grannycraft

I cut back the Golden Rod
which came from your garden,
and find the wands
that magic me to the under-world
of your glorious creations.

Here come all the boys and girls
who swallowed orange pips:
see those fresh shoots bursting
through ears and nostrils and skulls
into God's good light;

here too the Gormless Swots,
brains worn out by too much reading;
the Tribes of Midgets
who did not eat up all their greens;
legions of the unspeakable Blind;

and the Lockjaws, dumb and starving,
who played with sharp knives
between thumb and forefinger;
the Walking Gargoyles
who got none of their beauty sleep;

the Ham Fisted, whose sticky fingers
dropped off to dance in Hell;
and the Lost Souls who did not believe
that God can only be eaten on an empty stomach.

And here you are in the midst of them,
restored to your full floral XOS,
eyes saying sadly *I told you so*
and daring me to suggest
that you are almost winking.

Wayside Flowers

Preserved for Rural Studies, School Lane
still speaks of you Gran, eloquent
in the half-secret Language of Flowers;
its daisies breathe *innocence*,
coltsfoot *mothers' love*,
cream-white clover *think of me* —
which I do: the fragile *grief* of harebells,
consolation of red poppies,
each flower in its season.

But those which appear today
on the hard verge of the Urban Clearway
against a buckled crash barrier
are all suffocating in cellophane:
blue iris meaning *a message*,
blood-red chrysanthemums *love*,
the shop-soiled *purity* of white lilies,
calculated dozen rosebuds,
everything out of season.

I read those poisonous *can-you-helps*
appealing for eye-witnesses; and yes
I can see it only too well
but no, I can't help as I drive past
to collect another generation
from school, troubled by *forget-me-nots*,
rosemary for *remembrance*, your face,
and the whole Company of Heaven
and Hell back in season.

Spillover

A trolley overload topples
into the aisle, and images —
as elusive at first
as the spirit of a fresh corpse —
rise from the wreckage
as glass daggers pierce gherkins
and blackcurrant jam,
releasing smells which combine
with those from a swirl-pool
of ketchup, eggs and ginger ale.

Suddenly I am back on tiptoe
in Grandfather's corner grocery
in which the only true categories
were *dry* — scooped into brown bags,
and *wet* — slurped into old bottles,
and am wallowing in a childhood
in which few things were seal-packed
one from the other. I fancy
that the past, like the future,
is largely conjured up by accident.

But smart lads soon sift the worst,
and their SuperVac sucks the rest
into oblivion, leaving
only an aerosol whiff
of Gran's good-night lavender kiss
and a yellow Health and Safety
CAUTION : WET FLOOR
which alerts me — as I pick my way
through these systematic shelves —
that memory thrives on muddle

Sweet, savoury; fresh, frozen;
fish, fowl, good red meat;
but I am still struggling
to get into good and proper order
stewed tea, pilchards, apple scrunch,
sirens, snug shelters, syrup of figs,
girls' lips, dry books, wet dreams,
weddings, funerals, Mum, Dad,
and folk I am not, to be honest,
dying to met again.

The Spell

'On the *qui vive* now' whispers Uncle
lifting me from the oily fug of his van
high into the chill moonlight, the heath
impassive, waiting on the promise
of my first flying saucer hunt.

We stand half way between the owl
and its echo, slowly examining the night
until I know that I, too, am out in space,
that the sky does indeed start at my feet.
The air itches, the hands of my watch

nearly stop, my nostrils fill
with some vastly travelled smell like
the devilish salmon Uncle once caught
and laid out on the moss; eyes sting,
ears burr like a cold in the head,

and something faintly luminous touches
on the horizon, whispers to me
in vague night words, then vanishes,
leaving only a dentist-deadened tongue
and a mighty sense of inconsequence.

Back in the van, I share Uncle's cocoa,
his certainty that some craft has landed
on the edge of my blind spot, and, *qui vive*,
open a door for the spirit of the thing
to return to its own space.

Gloria in Violet

'She's got a tongue on her that one' warned Mum,
and Gloria did indeed speak her young mind
in the playground and on our street beyond,
broadcast choice words for the rudest of things,

and once opened wide to show that wicked tongue
streaked violet, fluttering like the wing tip
of the tropical bird Dr McKie had called 'thrush'
and painted *jenshum violent* — to match, she swore,

her knickers which she'd prove in the Church porch
at one Woodbine per peep. Danny reported
that they were thick navy like his sister's,
Ben that they were grey (him being colour-blind),

while I, sight unseen, accepted her word for it
preferring to spend my precious fag on a kiss,
tongue to tongue, wing tip to wing tip,
one exotic bird flitting from throat to throat —

which did it. A week later Dr McKie told Mum
there was an epidemic, as if half the kids
had been eating earth like poor Bartholomew,
27, and only let out to play at dusk

which is when I glimpsed our Gloria,
soft-hearted for the whole of mankind,
giving him a free one and trying to teach him
a new game called 'feelies'. I was cured;

but those unexamined *violet knickers,* pure words
less sullied than plain things, stick in my mind,
inviolate, on the tip of my tongue, erotic
beyond wives and all the infirmities of time.

Let Me Count the Ways

Laughter is the tickle of air
in your first attempt to kiss my ear;
it is helter-skeltering two abreast
that night at Skegness.

Laughter is you and me and the bolster
in that squeaky four-poster;
it's five-finger exercises on your spine
and your sixth sense at the wrong time.

Laughter is another seven years of itch,
an octopus we can't quite catch,
all nine muses out to play,
ten commandments loosely obeyed.

Concordance

About your *maybe* as we drift
the way of sleep, indeterminate
between the epic *yes* of youth
and the *no* that would deny a death:

think of all the other words we might

recover, try to pronounce with the same
chords. Remember how — at the third stroke —
Aunt Jodie's eyes were speechless too?
your mother's innocent *see you* at the end?

I think of all the other words I might

recover to incinerate, harmless in ones,
like *wish* and *I* and *never*,
but banded together stopping up your ears,
lethal perhaps. Don't go to sleep:

words are being re-arranged:

they say a 7th Generation main-frame
could — if minded — at a stroke
compile a full concordance
of the British Library, *aabec* to *zyzoo*.

Maybe there isn't any word that's past

recovery: a sentient 7th after that
might trace to source the faint disturbance
created for ever in the air we breathed
by even the most indefinite of our articles

and make some sense of us from all our words:

the changing contexts of such nouns as *touch*
and *time* and *bed*; adjectives which shrank from
hyperbole; the frequency and distribution
of the verb *to love* . . .   Stop:

I'm trying to touch you with words again.

But how can I love without vocabulary?
And somewhere there are words we haven't got
in proper order yet. See, this is called *a hand*
and it is used to soothe the language.

The Lock

Puttering upstream on another late summer treat
we ease our way into this slipshod lock
located somewhere between Lower and Upper Nowhere,
tether to shaky stanchions, and take stock

of the silence, the rusting mechanism,
and the time left to us. We heave,
it gives, and we leap back aboard to steady things
as the gush and swirl drowns out the weir we've

just avoided. Gradually, now, the way ahead
lifts into view, much the same
as we left behind though round the next curve
we may yet find elephants, a steel band, champagne,

a memorable sunset in which to slip away,
a fine and private mooring, and another day.

General Registry

All here: haunted girls scarcely come of age
to trace their birth mothers, Cheap Day trippers
grafting flesh onto family trees: the final
Great Grandfather half sighted in Auntie Vi's
wedding photos, the first wife born somewhere
in Rutland; divorced men taking time out
to sniff the ashes of old flames; slack-eyed
figures loitering by next year's empty shelves,
the homeless browsing among family remnants.

Here everything is accounted for, indexed,
colour-coded: live births red and screaming;
marriages green, fading; black death. The dust
has no time to settle, arms and elbows
clamouring for their ponderous muniments
tightly bound in the token dignity
of leatherette. The raw material
for bureaucrat and recording angel lies
just beyond this waiting room for purgatory.

I am here to meet a friend: arrive early:
wander into the quarter of my birth
amused yet reassured to find myself still
in their books: male child, St Luke's Hospital;
onto the Payments Counter, the Scale of Fees
offering cut-price copies for the purposes
of the Friendly Societies Acts. I am lost
in all this furious curiosity,
the desperation. Perhaps you are not coming.

I wait by the entrance. Here comes everybody
else: every face reflects something of you
or me — but never enough. I turn back,
rejoin this haunting of the query dead,
a Displaced Person searching row after row
of cots, deranged beds, gravestones: a place for
everything and everywhere just a place.
Beyond the revolving doors the floor polish,
rank and official, permeates my clothes.

Prompt

He freezes: time stretches. 'Life' I hiss:
'Life!' he declares, 'You don't know the meaning . . . '
and they are back to their set-piece wrangle
with me still safely out of sight.

The task is to keep my finger
on exactly the right word, while half my mind
struggles to re-write this pitiful script
and we plod to yet another curtain call.

I am tempted, next time, to slip you
the odd unauthorised word, dare you
to create your own dialogue, try to steer things
towards a slightly different ending.

Beyond Westminster Bridge

The man in the boiler suit carting bleach
to the top floor washrooms of NatWest Tower
alone saw the rainbow over Chelsea Reach
drift towards Westminster Bridge — as if drawn
to a curve almost as natural as its own —
then hover and, in the next bright shower,
settle onto the roadway, cutting a swathe
through the morning rush hour, which it bathed

in perfect colours. Alone he rang the *Sun*
who spiked him as another schizo case
as, on the Bridge, commuters inched ahead, none
sensing the glory about them, or taking delight
even in the unexamined uncut light
which fell on dull and soulless faces,
glinted on Thames and Embankment, marked
the debris of the City, penetrated the dark

foundations of the City's splendour. Alone
he rang the Commons where a few M.P.'s,
exhausted by overnighting, cursed the phone,
glanced at the Bridge, saw nothing save
bleary bands of red and blue — but braved
the air to dance in these to please
the Whips. Alone he sighed, scanned each
miraculous colour one last time, still craved
the prism, turned to his job, applied the bleach.

Local Democrat

Wednesday evening, *Parks and Cemeteries*,
and he's in the Public Gallery again,
roped off, alone, this nameless male
30-odd in egg-stained anorak, myopic specs,

who comes to *Highways, Amenities*, the lot,
sits silently night after night through potholes,
bye-laws, wayleaves, statutory nuisances, rats,
struggles with vast agendas to find his place.

If others venture into those hard seats
they keep their distance, slip away early,
never return; the Press may saunter in late,
ignite a debate and retire to the pub;

he alone persists, January through July
always wrapped tight, marmite sandwiches
not quite Sufficient Cause to have him ejected:
it's as if he's waiting for *his* item to come up.

I, the clerk, wonder: nobody talks with him
though speechifying Councillors
do increasingly try to catch his eye, downcast
as he earnestly noses the small print

hoping to connect this with all the wordy wisdom
and ritual disputatiousness
which rebounds from pomp-and-walnut walls
only to sink into their immemorial leather.

Don't give up Sir. We need you, our unknown voter
and silent witness; our representative too —
perhaps (being of no known party) the best.
And drains and things *do* matter.

The Traveller

Stranded between flights, bellyful of coffee,
he haunts anonymous lounges, driven to read
Instructions In Case Of Fire, then lights upon
a discreet sign **To The Chapel**,

ventures along half-hidden passageways
to a padded door, and this neat little room,
soundproofed from take-offs and panic,
uncommitted save to some general-purpose God

maintained in case of terror or unthinkable
disaster, meanwhile confined here,
with sensible beechwood chairs, flowers,
the multi-lingual **Invitation To Pray**

for which hassocks would be considered
far too controversial. No Bible for vandals,
no candle for fire-raisers, the stained glass
safely abstract, reaching only vaguely upwards.

He pauses. It seems a good place for a nap.
So why hesitate? Fear of getting locked in
by Security? Something worse? He slips away
fingers crossed for take-off.

Concerto for 3 Girls and Double Escalator

Again today, hanging out somewhere between school
and hope, they chatter onto the Concourse, free
of baggage or destination, simply
to cruise the escalators between Arrivals
and Departures, sky-larking on the brink of flight.

Together at first, borne up by such seemingly
endless purpose, the drone and fidget of treads
no longer quite at ease on their bearings,
they infiltrate the passengers, miming disbelief
at the security cameras. I should act

but it is time for the first solo. The Gymnast
locates a gap, seizes the parallel rails
quivering as she leans into the movement
and executes two three-quarter body rotations
before landing lightly on the lower floor

where each stair vanishes into the teeth
of the underworld. She turns, poised, defiant,
and hurtles herself against the downward thrust,
almost gaining the top, but a fraction's pause
and she slips away, lost. I should switch off

but the Dancer is already aboard, pirouettes
down, down, while the Japanese hoist their Nikons,
marks time behind an Arab lady with excess
hand luggage, waltzes back a few stairs
for a triumphant glissade onto terra firma

then takes a series of theatrical steps and joins
the Up. At once she drops in a heap, a sick cygnet,
slowly stretches, her body exaggerating
the routine rise, upstretched arms reaching for
the sky, moulding the air to her own will,

while the third, the Sensor, stands on the edge
of embarrassment, reacts to the flashing light
of the monitor, her imagination flying
to terrors being planned up here in Security.
She holds her ground, pleads time to go,

but is caught up for the final movement
to street level, each pitted against the others
and the determination of the escalator.
The flight to Paris is announced. It is a trifle.
Too late. The girls have flown again today.

Plain Words

Your Voices return. *Talk to me again* you say.
Chatting can sometimes shut them out. It's 1 a.m.
Plain words may drive the worst away.

Tonight at least you're not quite sure that they
Are real. I talk, they fade, but then at 2 a.m.
Your Voices return. *Talk to me again* you say.

I natter on about the things you've done today:
Got up, gone shopping, watched TV. It's 3 a.m.
Plain words may drive the worst away.

Another pot of tea for two. Must not betray
Despair, exhaustion, even when, at 4 a.m.
Your Voices return. *Talk to me again* you say.

I love you I whisper. *This is your home, to stay
As long as I can manage.* Now, though, it's 5 a.m.
Plain words may drive the worst away

Thank God. You go to bed. I try to sleep. No way.
Another night. Another day. It's 6 a.m.
Your Voices return. *Talk to me again* you say.
Plain words may drive the worst away.

Changing Day

Alone in the bedroom she struggles
to change the cover of a double duvet,
stripping the pink floral (soiled only
by time and nightmares) — child's play
once she'd got a grip on the innards
and heaved — but meeting deeper trouble

with a crisply-laundered reticent design
of interlocking oblongs, triangles,
squares, in which tocram a sprawling mass
of puffed-up matter now entangled
here in her arms — the task somehow to guess
the top and bottom of it all, then re-align

the thing. One hand, wriggling free, makes
a grab for the corner she believes her own
but her arms are never wide enough
to reach the other, and — facing alone
a four-hand task — she curses the stuff,
seizes on anything, and furiously shakes.

Memorabilia

You will apologise for me, say
I was nobody, just some man
caught up in your snaps of a littered beach
or overspilling pavement café,
a careless film extra, or at most
part of the background colour
in my holiday garb.

But these exposures feel more than accidents
for I dodge behind sunshades, merge into foliage,
yet you still manage to capture
some fragment of me — an outstretched hand,
sandalled foot, quiff of beard,
even a full frontal shadow.

It is as if I were not merely
a stranger, a fellow-pilgrim
to those sun-raked holy-lands,
but a putative saint
whose relicts you lift to Northern cities
preserved in fine caskets against X-ray tests
of my authenticity.

I have tried the disguise of a true sinner
fixing myself an alcoholic filter
till your image of me blurs;
tried when small enough to ward you off
by acting the gargoyle;
but always, everywhere,
you kept me in your line of sight.

I speak to you now, say
I am all and only human,
not even an idol for you to covet
a clump of hair or shred of underwear,
and I want back
those irreplaceable snips of me
secreted in your cupboards and attics.

I fear that in too many places
I have already been laid to rest
preserved like a withered flower
in your neglected black books,
my features flattened indecently
against the bosom of your family
to die and fade as strangers.

But could I piece together
what has already been taken?
Identify which bits are me? Or end
like the Old Man of Clacton
braced by 5-year old grandfather
who cannot now remember
whether he was somebody or nobody?

Pastoral

Browsing on the inconsequential rural bridge
he gazes down on the purposeful lanes of the M6 —
all those racing cars, brand-blazing lorries, Express coaches,
accelerating to and from the distant city —

unwraps another humbug high above the skid-marks
recording another bit of excitement which he missed —
the beer cans, packs of Marlboros, those shocking pink tights,
something else between an oily rag and a decomposing cat —

and rehearses a few choice lines of Pope as he reflects
on intersections purpose-built never to connect —
while a car-phone reports that he is just standing there
contemplating, surely, some terrible leap from freedom.

Night Line

Time-stretchers, we are here again
in case: moon shadows, coffee grouts,
the suppressed screams of telephones.
I am hearing voices, straining,

insubstantial, spaced-out, bereft
of loved and loathed familiars,
trapped in the yawning hours, tiring
of time, of whatever is left

before they're done: nightmares, night lines,
life lines. Still it is a question
of seeing things through. Day may break
the spell.

The Atlantic bellows,

soaks me sheltering,
splits driftwood into rare gifts.

I am a pebble-pond
furious for rocks;

I am a lake:
make me an Ocean;

pack me a hurricane
for home.

Palette

Let's start with flame-red and lobster and dragon blood;

let's add ochre and old gold and beaten copper,

    topaz, cadmium, brimstone and sulphur;

try jade, emerald, and aquamarine,

    sapphire and cobalt and peacock;

add deep dark indigo,

    amethyst, fuchsia, and gentian violet.

Let's invent fusion.

    And let it be good.

Henry Moore, 'Maternity'

(on loan to the NSPCC)

for Jim Harding

In the beginning, observe
the baboon and the Buddha
wholly at one. Here in Leeds
the Trustees know the limits
of trust, and set armoured glass
between their graven image
of a son given to the world
and all manner of deeds
by human hands.

In the third dimension
the entity itself scales down
to the cradle of a palm.
Senses swell. We capture
the grossness of fingers
which must fondle all new flesh
as it emerges from rock
or the rough passage to assumed calm
in man-made harbours.

'In some of my early work'
he writes, 'there is no neck
simply because I was frightened
to weaken the stone' — the substance
of the world, saved from abuse
or the mindless erosion of neglect
to yield this inheritance
of stranded muscle, gulleys —
riches from wrecks.

In stone, she holds hard. Consider
the art of reproduction
by simple cell division —
how the image is enlarged
by the power of mind —
the patient easing apart
of time — yet the chance that commits
or permits the mutilation
of her self.

In the end, observe the Aztec
and all the tribes of Africa
in our own flesh and stone
complete. Then, perhaps, one Mother
bearing a Child of such abundance
as to reconcile separation
and indivisibility:
mother-child, body-head, man-God.
And work to be done.

Five Swimmers

You should have seen us larking on the river
that first summer of freedom, no longer trapped
in the heavy stone slabs of school —
how we'd fling the girls in again and again,
plunge after them, grasp at legs and arms,
discovering a communal rhythm
like a quintet of cream-pink fish.

Maybe you noticed us in October
using our first Giro-chits as free passes
into the Municipal Swimming Baths
where we teamed up again day after day,
glad that there was nothing
in the factories or warehouses
to break into the time which was in our hands.

That's how we put this act together
creating something new in Showbiz
and imagining we might make it
like Torvill and Dean, learning by practice
the meaning of tangents, axes, parabolas,
until we achieved an impression of such ease
as limb reached for limb and for light.

We surfaced with talk of leaving town,
the tedium of parents, heavy figures
burdened with work and flab and possessions,
to perform in all the waters of geography —
the Great Lakes, Nile, Ganges,
Pacific, Orinoco, Titicaca,
trading in delight and acclaim.

But by Christmas this man David Wynne —
a sort of Employment Creation Supervisor —
talked of openings in the service industries
and cast us here in the Shopping Mall —
'Training for careers as Sculptees' —
in a fixed posture of freedom,
frozen as we merely pretend to go round and round,

round and round, round and round, aimlessly,
our eyes sealed from the brief glances
of bored and busy consumers, abandoned
to feel blindly for some contact with each other
like the gassed Infantry
in Smudger's battered history books,
and only the familiar voice of Miss Pringle —

who nagged us with Shelley and Keats,
and who is heading today for thermal tights
in British Home Stores — muttering
'Poetry, pure Poetry . . . '

David Wynne: *Five Swimmers*
in the Elmsleigh Centre, Staines

Shelf-Filler

I study the lean face
in my hand, the yellowing bust
of a young man which I wash
with care as if a prize
for archaeology,
and offer back rejuvenated
with skull-white emulsion
to the high shelf from which
he has eyed me for some 20 years.

These days friends often ask
if this is me when younger,
and I do not find it difficult
to imagine that heady hair
receding into mine,
that firm forehead (whose cracks
I have skilfully filled)
settling for my own furrows,
his future compelled by my past.

Yet when I was closer to his age
friends could never make out
who he was, with his strong bones,
hungry cheeks, formal collar,
blank eyes staring out
in hope or fear —
a minor Georgian poet perhaps,
or First World War subaltern.

Then I would explain
that he was just a shelf-filler
bought for 50p
at the Old Peoples Day Centre,
made in Occupational Therapy
by a spinster lady
whose arthritic hands
moulded from memory, again and again,
this single young man.

Mask to Maker

You struggle with fine mesh
giving me shape, wallow
in slip and slurry for my skin,
strain to quicken me, bend me to your will.

You feel for me: fingertips
rest on my forehead, palms hug
the contours of my cheeks, thumbs
snuggle behind my ears. I know hunger

in that touch. I feel your breath
all over me but my lips
stay icy, my skin numb, my self
immune from your urgings: I will not come

for you, am still changing shape,
fighting to become someone — like you —
despite your determination
to make some thing of me. My God, loosen

your grip: wicked fingernails
now rasp on paper-thin skin,
fists pound cheekbones, thumbs
poke into eye sockets. Stop. You're hurting

us both: see, you tore at my wires
and I slashed you. Plaster yourself,
let me be: I'm already
more than yesterday's news, have

your blood in me. Study
my features and find your kid
brother, your tortured twin,
your penile extension. Your alter id.

Home Viewing

Somebody should warn the fat lady
smug in her black and greying deck-chair
smoking. This early film is so flammable
that one spark could destroy everything:
    that dry laurel hedge, the crisp cotton
    of the picnicking girls, the baggy boys
    leapfrogging the lens, the whole guessed
    family, gardener, poodle, all eyeing us
as they jerk over the teeth of my spindle.

We can only identify the maid —
my neighbour's late aunt — called outdoors
to mime a fictional maid, tripping over
acres of lawn with a silver-plated note:
    the fat lady reads fast — every second
    precious on this spool. Clutches brow.
    Enter stage vicar, grinning. Snatches
    of boy scouts, clowns in Ford, man in fez.
Pan to Pageant, brief shadow of the tripod.

Curiosity is soon overwhelmed
by certainty. The fat lady, somewhere
in her own mid-thirties, has slipped away
purloining the script. I fetch her back —
    muddled in reverse, astonished
    by the sudden hypnosis, silent
    under close examination,
    without even the chitter of animation —
and I feel driven to shock her into sense.

I try telling her frankly that she is dead
and she does seem to give a slight flicker
though I know she will soon forget the fact
until something or other triggers it
    so release her, and she wanders in and out
    giving some private meaning to it all
    while still playing to this her public,
    clutching the dog, staring out,
mouthing 'good boy' or 'good bye' or something.

After Browning

'I was three parts through it when called to assist a servant to whom a strange
accident, part serious, part ludicrous, had suddenly happened; and after a
quarter of an hour's agitation, of a varied kind, I went back . . .'
— Robert Browning on the writing of *Transcendentalism*

I'm lying here just as I lived
Responsible for dust and things below,
Unsure, uncertain, hopeless, not allowed
To work on harps or anything resplendent.

I should be grateful: I suppose
That literary footnotes — albeit brief
And leaving one without a name (or sex) —
Last longer than corporeal descendents.

I should be sorry: I supposed
That I was merely flesh and so much blood
(Which Master relished more upon the page
Than emanating from a mere attendent).

I should explain now — if I could —
How such a signal part got trapped in that
Unspeakable contraption just as he
Had three parts captured his transcendent.

If only I'd not screamed so much
As he was struggling with the poet's task
(With 'plants could speak' and 'song's our art')
Rejecting all he called the 'transcendental'.

For if I was honest — more or less
The help he gave was generous with words,
(And though he urged 'hold hard' and 'be a man'
I think his choice of phrases accidental).

And if I'd agitated less
I might have gained a little insight, seen
The ludicrously serious in verse,
Beyond the self, the crudely fundamental —

And though cut short might still transcend
That strange, prosaic, bloody end.

Poetess

'I don't see what's wrong with a cliché'
Scowls the girl at the back of the Class:
'You know where you are with a cliché' —
And she glares at me — bold as brass.

She's planning to be a poet,
Has already done *God* and *My Guy*;
She knows where she is with a cliché —
Clear as crystal, straight as a die.

'If you don't like my *spring lambs a-frisking*
Then what would *you* put there instead?
And my friend here says what you call clichés
Are the best bits of poets that's dead.'

Half of the class think she's right there,
And the other half's too bored to reach,
Don't care where they are with a cliché
As she sticks to her guns like a leech.

77 — 81 Blue

Finding this strip of raffle tickets
in a party-best pocket
I recapture the sight of Eva Perkins
heading to claim her chocolate liqueurs
and imagine that something rich
might yet be won from tiny failures.

I could wallpaper the dolls house;
make five origami bluebirds
for a bonsai tree; punch out confetti;
start a lifetime collection
of pure numbers; haunt cloakrooms,
claim a rich man's coat.

Or I could stick with the ones I've got,
contemplate some mystic meaning
locked in the digits, and if I despair
could ticker-tape them from my window
or press one upon you in the street
with a smile and *may it bring you luck*.

Perhaps I could start a tiny fire.

The Invigilators

Finals: this is the end. Enter
another generation, anxious, jaunty,
names and numbers checked into ranks
as orderly as any military cemetery.
'You may start now': settle for silence,
lapse into a fidget of feet, sighs,
the odd snuffle, scrape of a chair,
spasmodic throats, rustling of sweets.

We are the barely visible presences,
retired for ages, found in the archives
to pass between you on soft footsteps,
breathing over you, fierce and kindly;
the shades discreetly patrolling even
your private places, alert for formulae
secreted in the graffiti, noting
your paper horseshoe, soggy, floating.

You avoid our eyes, your heads bowed
in obeisance to gods of lost causes
or gazing heavenward for answers
to the most unlikely of questions;
you race a clock which for us
seems to have stopped; you seize
on some new idea, frantic for more paper:
we have vast supplies of blank sheets.

'You have twenty minutes left'. We detect
a distant ambulance siren while
you scratch for that hairsbreadth of a pass
banging your head against an invisible wall;
our allotted time is almost up:
the first squeak of digital quartz
tempts a shaft of sun through a high window
and, perhaps, those precious few last words.

'You may finish the sentence you are
writing.' You gather yourself together
and slip away, free for a space, leaving
some account of yourself, the usual debris;
we bundle everything neatly away,
sign for our dues, pocket the expenses;
you take no memory of our faces;
we vanish for ever, unexamined.

Field Marshal

'It's nice for gentlemen to have a hobby, though they do gather the dust,
those skulls and things.'
— Mrs Haines in Virginia Woolf's *Between the Acts*

For Ray Stratford — Headmaster Plenipotentiary (retired)

They age in Wisden, embrace the world view
of Bradshaw or Stanley Gibbons, cling with a passion
granted only to the old;
                          love their gods
and their fellow-enthusiasts — jazz men or golf men,
devotees of Janes or the Beano;
                             trek to distant parts
to huddle and be happy only among flocks of twitchers
or where peony shall speak only to peony;
                                return
only to bore away at real neighbours
in this, the Most Ancient Order of Filibusters.

It is as if man's final life task is to grow
apart, to endure and enjoy a trial separation
with shrunken skulls and things.

But *you* are ageing with all the brilliance
of the primary child, the snapper-up
of endlessly considered trifles
                          from Aardvark
to the Zuyder Zee, as you blow the dust
from Entomologist and Etymologist,
                           cajole
Everyman and his Fiend in the real language
of our kind,
                     gleefully change hobby-horses
in mid-stream in your enthusiasm for life itself
and its God.

It is as if your task now is to muster
all those incorrigible Privates: you the General,
Field Marshal of the Essex Marshes.

Marginalia

They walk the coastal strip at cooler hours,
comfortable figures with long winter leases
on southern sun, deny the parched beauty
of the interior, see beyond their harbour
nothing but white breakers as, day on day,
foibled by years, they pace the margin
between lethargy and careful luxury —
men who were once somebody, and women
who were once somebody's wife, squeezing
into quickly whitewashed developments
maintaining a fine line between fantasy
and futility, neither home nor away,
awaiting sunset and evening star
to cross, very slowly, to Manuel's Bar.

A cheapish end as they bury themselves
out there, trenches for further white slabs?
Or did I see things that do not quite lie
between death and resurrection, stirrings
in personal columns — *Apprende Espanol:
learn what your neighbour is saying* —
and bright eyes in ravaged faces, eager?
But then I was only a quick winter break
between ice and work and ice and work,
an ageing word-processing middleman
still vulnerable when the Time Share touts
pounce, trading on their strip of shining
sand, over-ready to assay the silver
with which decent people line their lives.

Winter Tale

I don't set out to read your love letters,
tax returns, family trees, study notes,
summonses, schedules of securities:
but when you leave them in the copier
who could help being curious?

I'm no thief. I always put them back
when I've finished: the recipes, plans,
pools coupons, workshop manuals, profiles
of stars; but as I trudge home I envy
the variousness of other lives.

You queue day after day for something
more purposeful than the winter warmth
in which I loiter, but as you head off
I curse if you remember to take the lot,
may copy any prize piece which you forget.

I have studied the Rules of Reproduction
and you can't copyright a life. Look to
your originals: if there's a gap
I may have a duplicate. I am a collector
beyond trifles: I specialise in last pages.

Once a month or so I still light upon
some new end: curtain down on an unknown
play, a diabolical conclusion put upon
an essay, an obituary as scarcely bloodied
as the last (not to be forgotten) tampon.

Soapscapes

It's not easy even with everyday bath slabs
packed four-square, smelling serviceable,
chunky enough to grasp firmly, hard-skinned,
disinclined to sogginess, yet forever

slithering into the water; more difficult
now that my eyesight clouds over too
and gently-nudged limbs aren't nimble enough
to twist in an instant; almost impossible

with this little gift, its rare scent,
gentle action, deep-skin promise,
curvaceous and slippery as a tropical fish
which escapes me at the slightest touch,

vanishes into its own slipstream,
neither sinks nor floats, suspended
between here and nowhere, unable to settle,
infuriating me with its vague presence

as I thrash around, sense and lose it
again and again, try absolute stillness
in which it only lurks in absolute silence
to dissolve into a shapeless nothing. But

I refuse to let this small gift go to waste,
resume casting about, and feel something
adrift in the swell, inanimate and wayward
as the drowned.

Findings

At the back of the shed I have found
the gate-leg table at which I proposed;
last year, in the Museum of Transport,
I happened upon the self-same taxi
which jolted us to bed: the brittle leather,
my restless silence, your honeymoon scent.

Last Christmas, on the late night movie,
Doris Day was wearing your pink polka-dot,
while last month, in the Woolworths sale,
I salvaged a lusty tradescantia
suspiciously like the first one we perched
on the bathroom windowsill of No. 74.

Last week I spotted a tiny silver shoe
secreted among your earrings. Yesterday
the computerised library ticket
which keyed you into a thousand novels
fell from your bedside locker with my photo,
these keys, the hospital recall card . . .

Wool in the Reckoning

Manacled to Mother Grandmother
by skeins of multi-ply, subjected
to taut commands — up a bit, don't *flop* —
mixed with scarcely answerable questions
about everything precious, I lied.

Under woollen blankets I dreamt that downstairs
methodical fingers were unwinding
those self-same balls ready to re-bind me,
submit me to further interrogation
until I snapped. I said *nothing*.

Aunts, Great Aunts, knitted my hands
into their mittens, came with shapeless kisses,
tested me with tongue-twisting riddles about
things, and left me unable to grasp anything
cleanly, all fingers-and-thumb dumb —

until I cast off the endless cable-stitch,
carted bin-bags of shrunken comfort
to the Hospice Shop, and cut free
of all things snug and woolly, all
products of impertinent love. Quietly,

I went all the way with man-made fibre,
harsher ready-to-wear synthetics,
tough viscose with slogans made up
by strangers, anything easy-care, easy-go,
won from extruded no-questions-asked sludge —

unaware that today, somewhat creased,
I would be slipping woollies over the stiff arms
of hard wearing old ladies, old old ladies,
eyes full of vague questions I do not answer.
Nor, however pertinent, do I ask —

What are you up to these days? Who do you think
you married? Do you still love Mummy? Where
are you going later? Do you sometimes get
feelings — you know — *feelings*? So what
are you going to do with the rest of your life?

Back home, feeling a chill in the air,
I rummage through my growing mix'n match —
them and us, his and hers, then and now,
pure wool and pure invention — for something
soft, warm, tough, and somehow *me*. And I sing.

Purple Testament

An answer to Jenny Joseph's *Warning* voted most popular post-1945 poem in a 1996 BBC poll.

Now that she is *really* old she wears one purple slipper
shuffling through the Ward looking for something vaguely
like the other, which she swears is red.
Her pension is assigned to the Unit General Manager
barely covering the incontinence pads and the laundry:
there is little left for the cost of living.
She accosts strange men who pretend not to be doctors,
drools over the heady white chrysanthemums
which her daughter has brought from the old garden,
then dribbles yellow-streaked petals which she refuses
to spit out.

She wears velcro skirts which won't quite stay up
now that she is so terribly thin;
she won't touch the poisoned food
but hoards breakfast crusts in her knickers.

I, now, have a job here to keep a roof
over my own head; somehow I don't swear
at God; I try to set a good example
for my own children; and I write the odd poem.

Maybe I ought to practice feeling ashamed of myself
while I can — as she might if she were *really* here
just playing with something purple.

Gibberish

Mocked by an idiotic name, Gibberish
thrived long before Babel and Bible,
is older even than *Ursprache*, remains
majestically free of dictionaries. It is

the sacred language of the profound;
the speech of orgasm, of babyish falterings,
of losing everything loved and more, of
shock and meltdown; grumbling of the Spheres;

howl of the sheeted dead rising to Caesar;
unheroic last words; wails and Wakes; talk
of the Devil; speak of tongues and of angels,
the vernacular of our own beast-brain;

the rant of the Sphinx, all Dutch, double
Chinese, and Greek whispers, pure vocables
and raw syntax; tough twaddle ripened
into mystery; the lingua franca of Lear,

of *hewgh* and *fitchew*, *squiny* and *falchion*;
of lost words and of the nonce words
we don't yet know we know. Gibberish
demands a hearing. I loosen my larynx

and launch from single words — *lixish*, say,
grinning at the camera, or *gorunder* shouted
at the overtaker — into a full length quest
for a *squillet* of wise fool's gold.

Can These Bones . . . ?

Here in the hospice, saints in the making
nurse endless souls on their shitty way
with quietly ferocious compassion.

Yet I worry about the Blessed Company
they might find in Heaven
given their excruciating niceness
to each other, the carefully constructed
pleasantries, the Changing Room where Sue
and Madge bicker for sole possession of
the precious last hours of patients who swear
'you must be a very special kind of person'.

Are all saints incorrigibly singular?
Or do these belong to a lower order
of bitchy angels? Perhaps
they are just choice mortals offered up young
to pacify Dragon Death, who then scorns
to dispose of them humanely, in one gulp,
but gnaws on them for year after year
until they are little more than bones

which we can, if we choose, revere as relics
but which will grate against the bones of others
whatever the company.

Ear Work

'The ear knows it all' says the acupuncturist,
her stylus circumnavigating the lobe,
easing its way into his coarsened pores,
probing, painless, until — the old man winces.

She swivels to an ear-chart, esoteric
as alchemy, traces the ancient pain-paths
back to the latest outcrop, fixes an ear-stud
for him to worry from time to time.

This patient will stab his own brain into life
until it despatches its anaesthetic
to the precise spot of the cancer. Listen.
The word is cancer. The ear is wise.

All Night Check-out

Night, day, it's all the same in the end,
a job, a pay packet, though somehow
people seem stranger in the small hours
and I wonder more about them,
where they come from,
                              where they're going.

And on nights, space seems vaster
the lulls more acutely silent,
our regular small dramas more intense.
We are here for everyday things
which won't wait.
                    I am here when you are ready.

Every night people arrive, back off,
whisper, try to make love of a sort,
feud, cry, see visions, talk to God,
depart. I rest my hand on the surface;
there is no magic eye:
                        no price will register.

House Hoard

This house acquires
things: umbrellas
with one broken rib,
last-gasp toothbrushes,
toothless combs,
scraps of strange letters
shoved down sofas,
chewed-up pencil stubs —
none of it ours.

This house has
kleptomania:
it steals odd socks
from anyone
with half a foothold here,
purloins lace hankies
screwed up
with enough germs
to finish us all off.

This house
will seize on perfume
secreting it
about its person
for months on end;
it spirits away
old family photographs
and sometimes, at 2 a.m.,
flashes them on the ceiling.

One night,
imagining I was out,
this house
briefly let slip
the cough my mother left behind
all of twenty years ago.

Glass, Darkly

These assorted Saints,
worked by some unremarked Victorian
into lead-heavy glass,
are good as dead,

the Ancient Lights
which willed them to glory in the sun
long stolen
by those blessed tower flats;

but one weary woman
still defies stale incense, rampant mice,
to stretch up
and wipe their grimy feet,

while behind her
one 15-watt star hangs over the Nativity
still aspiring
to floodlight the lot.